Spot the Difference

Flowers

Charlotte Guillain

Heinemann Library
Chicago, Illinois

Customer Service 888-454-2279
Visit our website at www.heinemannraintree.com

Designed by Joanna Hinton-Malivoire
Photo research by Erica Martin and Hannah Taylor
Printed and bound in China by South China Printing Co. Ltd.
12 11 10 09 08
10 9 8 7 6 5 4 3 2 1

The Library of Congress Cataloging-in-Publication Data
Guillain, Charlotte.
  Flowers / Charlotte Guillain.-- 1st ed.
     p. cm. -- (Spot the difference)
  Includes index.
  ISBN-13: 978-1-4329-0945-1 (library binding-hardcover)
  ISBN-10: 1-4329-0945-2 (library binding-harcover)
  ISBN-13: 978-1-4329-0952-9 (pbk.)
  ISBN-10: 1-4329-0952-5 (pbk.)
  1. Flowers--Juvenile literature. I. Title.
  QK49.G76 2008
  582.13--dc22
                              2007035749

Acknowledgements
The publishers would like to thank the following for permission to reproduce photographs: ©Corbis pp.**12**, **23 middle** (Craig Tuttle), **5** (Scot Frei); ©FLPA pp.**20** (Foto Natura/DUNCAN USHER), **14** (Minden Pictures/INGO ARNDT), **19** (Chris Demetriou), **21** (Holt Studios/Nigel Cattlin), **23 bottom** (Holt Studios/Nigel Cattlin), **6** (Nigel Cattlin); ©Getty Images p.**10** (TAUSEEF MUSTAFA); ©istockphoto.com pp.**4 bottom right** (Stan Rohrer), **4 top left** (CHEN PING-HUNG), **4 top right** (John Pitcher), **4 bottom left** (Vladimir Ivanov); ©Nature Picture Library pp.**8** (Andrew Parkinson), **15** (NEIL LUCAS), **9** (Philippe Clement), **11** (Ross Hoddinott), **16** (Ross Hoddinott); ©Photodisc pp.**13**, **22 right** (Hans Wiesenhofer); ©Photolibrary pp.**18**, **22 left** (Chris Burrows), **17** (David Dixon), **7**, **23 top** (Pacific Stock /Dahlquist Ron).

Cover photograph of flowers reproduced with permission of ©Photolibrary (Pacific Stock /Dahlquist Ron). Back cover photograph of dahlias reproduced with permission of ©Photodisc (Hans Wiesenhofer).

Every effort has been made to contact copyright holders of any material reproduced in this book. Any omissions will be rectified in subsequent printings if notice is given to the publishers.

Contents

What Are Plants?

Plants are living things.
Plants live in many places.

Plants need air to grow.
Plants need water to grow.
Plants need sunlight to grow.

What Are Flowers?

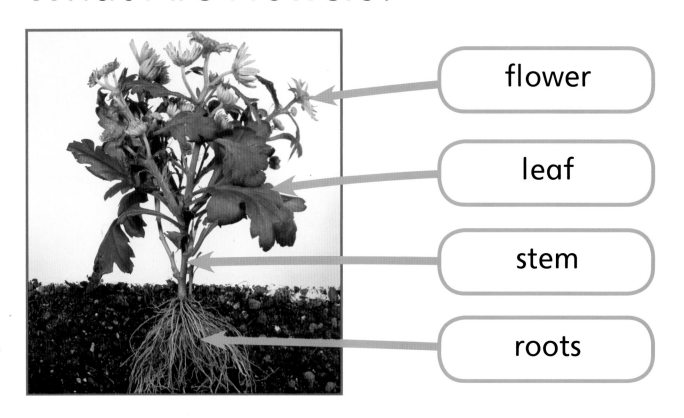

flower

leaf

stem

roots

Plants have many parts.

Many plants have flowers.

Different Flowers

This is a poppy.
Its flowers are red.

This is a viola.
Its flowers are blue.

This is a tulip.
It has one flower.

This is a primrose.
It has many flowers.

petal

This is a foxglove.
Its flower has one petal.

petal

This is a dahlia.
Its flower has many petals.

Amazing Flowers

This is a rafflesia.
It is a very big flower.

This is a titus arum.
It is a very tall flower.

This is a bumblebee orchid.
It looks like a bee.

This is a trumpet flower.
It looks like a trumpet.

This is a starflower.
It is a star shape.

This is a bluebell.
It is a bell shape.

What Do Flowers Do?

Flowers make seeds.

Seeds grow into new plants.

Spot the Difference!

How many differences can you see?

Picture Glossary

 **flower** the part of the plant that makes seeds

 **petal** part of a flower

 **seed** the part the plant that can grow into a new plant

Index

Note to Parents and Teachers

Before reading
Bring to class a collection of different flowers. Talk to the children about the flowers and ask them to name the different colors. Let the children smell the flowers and talk about why flowers are often bright colors or have a strong smell (to attract insects). Show them the different parts of the flower (petals, stamens, pistil).

After reading
• Place some flowers of different colors on a tray and show them to the children. Explain that you are going to cover the tray and take away one of the flowers. The children can guess which flower is missing.
• Show the children pictures of different flowers. Divide the children into groups of three or four and give each group a different flower. Ask them to identify parts of the flower, using their books as a guide.
• Make 3D flowers using different colored tissue paper. Fold a piece of tissue paper (approximately 8 inches square) into quarters. Draw a petal shape starting from the folded corner and away from the open edges. Cut out the shape. Unfold the petals, pinch the center of the flower and attach to a stick. Display the flowers in a jar.